# Smart Guess
## MYSTERY ADVENTURE

Think Social Publishing, Inc., Santa Clara, California
www.socialthinking.com

# Smart Guess
Mystery Adventure

Ryan Hendrix, Kari Zweber Palmer, Nancy Tarshis, Michelle Garcia Winner

ISBN: 978-1-936943-29-6 (print)
ISBN: 978-1-936943-77-7 (ebook)

Think Social Publishing, Inc.
404 Saratoga Avenue, Suite 200
Santa Clara, CA 95050
Tel: (408) 557-8595
Fax: (408) 557-8594

This book was printed and bound in the United States by Mighty Color Printing.
TSP is a sole source provider of Social Thinking Products in the U.S.
**Books may be purchased online at www.socialthinking.com.**

# Introduction to Storybook 7

We make a **smart guess** when we take what we observe and combine that with what we know. We consider the context/situational clues, people, their body language, tone of voice, etc. and make observations about who, what, and where we are. We then combine this information with our general knowledge about the way the world works coupled with any specific personal knowledge we have about the people around us to make a reasonable guess, prediction, or inference. By teaching students to make smart guesses, we help them learn to observe and become more aware of the world around them.

## We Thinkers! Our Amazing Early Learner Curriculum!

*We Thinkers!* Volume 1* - *Social Explorers* and Volume 2 - *Social Problem Solvers* is an engaging Social Thinking® series designed to teach Michelle Garcia Winner's basic Social Thinking Vocabulary concepts to children ages 4-7. Each volume consists of storybooks, curricula and kid-friendly music that make core social concepts come alive for young learners. The teaching is cumulative: Volume 1 helps prime students for the deeper social concepts and activities in Volume 2.

Volume 1 explores five basic social concepts that help children learn about the social world around them, and, to observe and think about others as they learn to be part of a group: *thinking thoughts and feeling feelings, the group plan, thinking with your eyes, body in the group, and listening with brain and body.* Volume 2 introduces five core Social Thinking concepts related to teaching stronger executive functioning in a classroom or group setting: *hidden rules and expected/unexpected behavior, making a smart guess, flexible versus stuck thinking, the size of the problem, and sharing an imagination.* Each storybook is aligned with a curriculum unit that breaks down these social emotional concepts into concrete, teachable segments. Adults find detailed strategies and explicit ways to engage students and foster deeper learning about each concept.

Our goal in developing the *We Thinkers!* series is to provide sequenced clear instruction to engage students in their own social emotional learning so they can become better group collaborators and problem solvers. To that end, in Volume 2 we introduce a Group Collaboration, Play and Problem Solving (GPS) scale, checklist and interactive play activities. These materials guide parents and professionals in evaluating each child's current abilities to relate to their peers and then choose from an array of interactive play activities based on their particular social learning needs.

While all children can benefit from the social emotional teaching that is at the foundation of our *We Thinkers!* series, it was specifically designed to help promote social learning in neurotypical or neurodivergent children who also have social learning differences (e.g. autism spectrum levels 1 and 2, ADHD, social communication differences or social anxiety, etc. or no diagnoses). However, mainstream teachers now adopt our materials for use with all students as they find them user-friendly for all.

* formerly titled *The Incredible Flexible You, Volume 1*

## Teaching the Curriculum, Concepts and Activities

What does play have to do with group collaboration and classroom learning? It is well documented in the research that interactive and pretend play is the avenue through which our young children practice and grow their social thinking and social skills. By the time children enter kindergarten it is assumed they have learned basic concepts and skills that allow them to work and learn academic concepts in a group setting.

It's tempting to think of play as simple, but it's actually a highly complex array of concepts and skills that work together simultaneously to enable a child to be successful in playing and interacting with others. Through interactive play children learn pivotal group interaction skills that will carry them through to adulthood. Play encourages the development of problem solving and conflict resolution skills, facilitates big-picture thinking, conceptual development, perspective taking, and executive functioning.

Our multi-sensory curriculum reflects the idea that learning should be interactive and playful. Activities involve using our eyes, ears, body and brain to make important social emotional connections. Teaching within the series draws on:

- "bibliotherapy" – using the words and illustrations in storybooks to help young learners develop an understanding of self and others and elicit a therapeutic response;

- "music therapy" – using music to help foster engagement around our core social emotional concepts;

- a wide range of activities to encourage children to explore and practice each of our 10 core concepts;

- "differentiated interactive play instruction" – not all children have the same abilities to play with other children. Through our GPS scale and checklist, parents and professionals can select which play activities are best suited to the child's level.

Together, the materials provided in our *We Thinkers!* series help young learners develop the five core competencies at the heart of social and emotional learning (SEL): self-awareness, self-management, social awareness, relationship skills, and responsible decision-making. The concepts marry playful, interactive learning to Common Core, state or country standards of education around the world.

## Pace Yourself and Your Kids!

The concepts in Volume 2 explore group collaboration at a deeper level and the ideas are a little more detailed to teach. To increase engagement and protect kids from becoming overwhelmed, we recommend teaching the stories in sections. While we encourage you to let your students guide you in determining the "best" places to start and stop, we've noticed in our own teaching more natural breaking points in the plot and content. These sections are outlined below and are marked in the story.

Section 1, pages 1-11: Introduce the Smart Guess formula

Section 2, pages 12-17: Example of making a smart guess; what is Molly's plan?

Section 3, pages 18-25: Making a smart guess about how Ellie is feeling

Section 4, pages 26-31: Making a smart guess about the group plan

The *We Thinkers!* series is available for purchase in the U.S. at www.socialthinking.com.

Evan, Ellie, Jesse and Molly are going to have a mystery adventure! But only Ellie knows what they are going to do. She has the plan in her brain.

Ellie thinks it would be fun for the other kids to guess what they are going to do together...but she doesn't give them any clues. They can't see what she's looking at in her backpack and Ellie is not saying anything. The kids could be about to do almost ANYTHING!

Sometimes we don't have enough information to make a **smart guess**. When we guess without knowing anything or having any clues, it is called making a **wacky guess**. Evan guesses they are going to cook in the kitchen, Jesse guesses they are going to do an art project, and Molly guesses they are going to play doctor. Ellie has a different plan.

| Look | Listen | Think |
|------|--------|-------|

It can be fun to make silly or wacky guesses, but it doesn't help us figure out the group plan. Ellie wants the kids to make a smart guess.

To make a smart guess we look, listen, and think. We use our eyes to gather clues, we listen to the words others are saying, and we think about the situation and what we might already know.

Stop and Notice

Ellie has a plan to help the kids make a smart guess about what they'll
be doing today. First she shows them some things from the backpack.
They see a hat, mittens, and a scarf.

The kids think about wearing the clothes in the kitchen, while painting, or at the doctor's office. Evan and Molly know they wear winter clothes when it's cold. You don't need warm clothes while cooking or playing doctor. That would be unexpected and wacky!

Evan and Molly will have to make a different guess about Ellie's plan.

Jesse is still thinking about painting.

His brain is stuck thinking about the art project and he thinks about painting while wearing mittens, a scarf, and a hat. Jesse is making a wacky guess! Painting in mittens would be very hard and would make a big mess!

Next, Ellie tells the kids she wants to make a snowman
on their adventure.

Evan and Molly hear Ellie talking about making a snowman. They know you need snow to make a snowman. They make a smart guess that their adventure is to play in the snow! Jesse is still stuck thinking about his art project... with a snowman. Hmmm... that seems kind of wacky.

| Look | Listen | Think |
|------|--------|-------|

Look, listen, think, go! Jesse uses flexible thinking. He thinks about what he sees, what he hears, and what he knows and makes a smart guess. Ah ha! They are going to play in the snow!

Stop and Discuss

10

The kids all wonder... is it a SNOW ADVENTURE?

Evan asks Ellie, "Are we going to play in the snow?"

What a smart guess! Yes! Now all of the kids know the group plan.

It's time to put on their snow clothes.

Evan, Ellie, Jesse and Molly look out the window at the snow.

Molly knows what she wants to do first.

Evan, Ellie and Jesse don't yet know Molly's plan.

Stop and Notice

Stop and Discuss

Molly wants the others to make a smart guess about her plan. Ellie and Jesse see Molly holding ice skates. They make a smart guess she wants to go ice skating. Evan is not looking at or thinking about Molly.

He guesses she wants to make a pizza. That's a wacky guess!
You don't make pizza in the snow!

Molly tells the kids she can't wait to race across the ice.

Evan hears this and thinks with his eyes to see Molly lacing up her skates.

| Look | Listen | Think |
|------|--------|-------|

Look, listen, think, go! Evan thinks about what he sees,

what he hears, and what he knows and makes a smart guess.

Ah ha! The plan is to go ice skating!

Ice skating was so much fun!
They walk over to get some hot cocoa.

THUNK – what was THAT?

Stop and Discuss

19

SNOWBALL

# FIGHT!

Molly is having fun throwing snowballs.

She hears Ellie yell, "Stop!"

Molly thinks with her eyes and sees Ellie is covered in snow and all wet.

A penguin throws another snowball. That's unexpected! If someone looks upset and says "Stop!" he or she does NOT want to play. The penguin did not use the clues he could see or hear to make a smart guess about how Ellie was feeling. He made a wacky guess she still wanted to play!

Stop and Discuss

| Look | Listen | Think |
|------|--------|-------|

Look, listen, think, go! Molly takes what she sees, what she hears
and what she knows and makes a smart guess.
Ah ha! Ellie wants to stop the snowball fight.

Stop and Discuss

Molly tells the penguin to stop.

He stops throwing snowballs and thinks about the hidden rules of snowball fights and how you have to think with your eyes and listen to what others are saying to make sure everyone is having fun. Oops! The penguin says, "Sorry Ellie!" The penguin changes his plan!

Molly remembers what Ellie talked about doing on their adventure.
Molly has an idea...

Stop and Discuss

Molly starts to roll one of the snowballs across the snow.

Jesse and Evan make a smart guess about Molly's plan and join in.
Evan asks the penguins to bring over a carrot, sticks, and a hat.

| Look | Listen | Think |
|------|--------|-------|

Look, listen, think, go!

What do YOU see? What do YOU hear?

What do YOU already know?

Make a smart guess! The group is making...

Stop and Discuss

A snowman!

On their adventure the kids learned how to make smart guesses about others' thoughts, feelings, and plans. Making a smart guess helps us know what to say and do and how others may be thinking and feeling. That helps EVERYBODY feel good about being together! Let's make a smart guess about what they will do next!